Exciting things to make with

paper

about this book

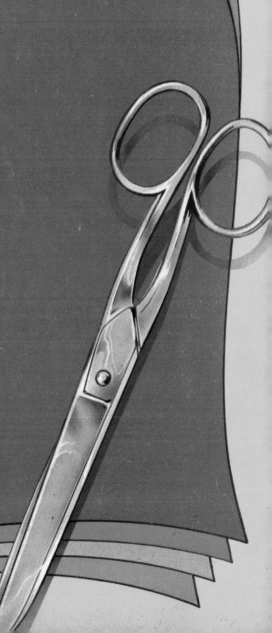

LOOK AND MAKE BOOKS are real do-it-yourself craft books. Every page has such clear step-by-step pictures and easy-to-follow words, that you can do everything on your own without adult help. And once you see how the projects work, you'll be inspired to make dozens of creative things!

This book is about things you can make with paper – simply by folding, cutting, twisting or sticking it. The chapters are arranged in a progression, with the easier projects at the beginning and the more difficult ones at the end. In many cases the methods in one chapter introduce the methods in the next chapter, so it's good idea to follow the order of the book.

The red tag at the side of the page tells you the method the chapter explains – all the projects between one tag and the next are all based on the same method.

The 'Try it first' tag at the top of the page indicates a practice section. This helps you to understand how a method works with a simple project, before starting on something bigger and more exciting. It also means you can experiment with odds and ends rather than using specially bought papers.

Before you start it's helpful to read through the Useful Things to Know pages that follow.

Paper

The projects in this book are made with all kinds of different paper. Although it is not absolutely necessary to use the kind of paper listed for each one, you will get better results if you do.

But before you go out to buy special papers, try doing the projects with odd bits of paper that you can find around the house.

Start collecting paper bags, supermarket shopping bags, used wrapping paper, newspapers, cereal boxes and other cardboard boxes and tubes – all of them will be useful.

When you are ready to buy paper, make sure you take careful note of how much and what kind of paper you need. Art supply stores have all the papers listed and can help you choose the right kind. A large stationery store may have some of the papers, such as tracing paper and stiff paper.

Cover paper is sturdy and holds a crease well. It is available at art supply stores in many colors.

Tissue paper is thin and flimsy and lets light through. It creases very crisply and is also easy to screw up into tight balls. You can't paint on tissue because the dye runs if it gets wet. Use tissue for making delicate things such as paper flowers.

Stiff paper that holds its shape includes index cards, file folders and heavy drawing paper. Where even greater firmness is needed, use lightweight cardboard.

Tracing paper is see-through: you will need it for all the projects that have trace patterns. If you want, you can use onionskin paper instead.

Construction paper is less durable than cover paper but it is also less expensive. It comes in colors too.

Gummed labels, the peel-and-stick type, come in various shapes, sizes and colors and are useful for decorating projects.

Things to remember

1. Try to store paper flat, so that it doesn't get crumpled.
2. If it does get crumpled, you can smooth it with a warm iron.
3. Keep all the scraps of paper left over from a project. You can probably use them for another one.

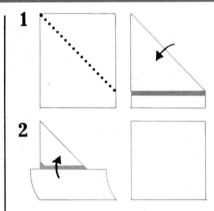

Before you start a project, read through the whole chapter first, so you have a picture in your mind of what to do. Then get together all the things you need. Refer to these pages if it helps. Clear yourself a large space and cover it with newspaper, so that it doesn't matter if you make a mess with paints or glues. Cover yourself up too with an apron or smock. Have an old cloth handy so you can clean your hands. When you've finished, always clear up blobs of paint and glue as quickly as possible. Roll up the newspaper with the messy side and all the rubbish inside and throw it away. Take care to put lids on properly and to wash brushes, bowls and other things you have used.

Square from a rectangle

1. Fold the top right-hand corner of the paper over to the left-hand edge, as shown.
2. Fold up the bottom edge along the line shown and make a crease. Cut along the crease. Open out the paper: it will now be a square.

Tools

Scissors

For most of your cutting ordinary household scissors will do. For delicate, careful cutting you'll need small pointed scissors too.

Pencils

Pencils are graded according to whether they are hard or soft. Look for the initial or number at the end of the pencil. H and 3 are hard; B and 1 are soft.

The most useful type is HB or 2. For tracing use a soft pencil and for drawing fine details use a hard one.

Glue

These are the four most useful types of glue. You can buy them at most stationery stores.

Paper paste. This is good for pasting thin paper such as tissue, because it dries clear. If you splash it on your clothes it will wash off with water.

White glue. This is stronger than paper paste and is the best kind of all-round glue for most of the projects. You can also thin it with water to use as a varnish. If you splash some on your clothes you must wash it out while it is wet: once it is dry it won't come out. Elmer's is one make of white glue.

Household cement. This is very strong, but it is quite expensive. Use it for making spots of glue which you want to dry very hard,

very quickly.

Rubber cement. Excess can be rubbed away easily, leaving no mess.

Cellophane tape

For most joins you can use tape which is sticky on only one side. If you want to make the tape invisible use double-coated tape.

Paints

Poster paints are the most useful to buy for doing these projects. They are mixed with water, and any spills can be cleaned up with water. You don't need to buy a whole range of colors: start with the basic ones – red, blue, yellow, black and white – and experiment with mixing.

Buy two or three paintbrushes, each of a different thickness. Use old lids, saucers or plastic eggboxes for mixing the paints in.

If you prefer, use felt-tipped pens instead of paints.

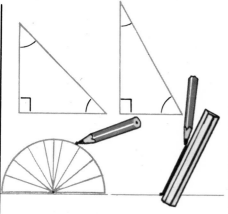

Measuring angles

There are two useful tools for measuring angles – a set square and a protractor. A set square can only measure three angles – 90° (a right angle), 60°, 30°, or 90°, 45°, 45° – but with a protractor you can measure any angle you want.

Drawing a circle

Set the arms of the pair of compasses so that the distance between them is the radius of the circle you want. Put the pin arm firmly on the paper, in the place where you want the center of the circle to be. Swing the pencil arm round to make a circle.

Finding the center

If you use a pair of compasses, the center of the circle is where you put the pin arm. If you draw round a cup or glass, use this method to find its center.

1. Draw a line across the circle.
2. Draw another line at right angles to this first line.
3. Draw in two more lines to make a rectangle.
4. Draw in the diagonals. The center of the circle is where these lines cross.

Parts of a circle

circumference

diameter

radius

1

2

3

4

cm

How to trace a pattern

Here are two ways of tracing and transferring patterns. Use the first method for tracing patterns in this book. They are all shown the wrong way round, so that they are the right way round when you transfer them onto paper. Use the second method if you want to trace a pattern from another book.

▶ You will need:
Tracing paper, pencil, tape and some scrap paper

1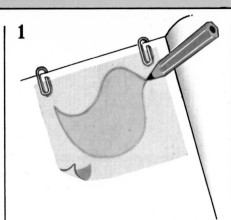

Method for this book

Remember – the trace patterns are the *wrong* way round and so your finished picture will be the *right* way round.
1. Lay tracing paper over the pattern and fix it to the page with paper clips.
Trace the outline of the pattern.

2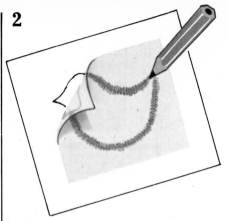

2. Turn the tracing paper over and scribble over the outline onto the paper you are using. When you lift the tracing paper you will find an outline of the pattern on it.
If the outline is too faint, draw round it again with a sharp pencil.

How to enlarge a pattern

For one or two of the projects you may want to make the patterns larger than they are shown in the book. You can enlarge them quite easily by following this method.

▶ You will need:
☐ Sheets of tracing paper
☐ Pencil
☐ Ruler
☐ Graph paper, preferably with large squares
☐ Tape

1

1. Trace the pattern you want to enlarge onto tracing paper.

2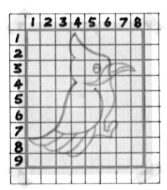

2. Lay the traced pattern over some graph paper and fix it in place with tape.
Draw a rectangle around the pattern, along lines on the graph paper.
Number the squares on two sides of the rectangle, as shown.

1

Another method

1. Lay tracing paper over the pattern and draw the outline of the pattern on it.

2

2. Turn the tracing paper over and put in on a piece of scrap paper. Scribble over the outline.

3

3. Put the tracing, right side up, on a clean sheet of paper and draw round the outline again.

3

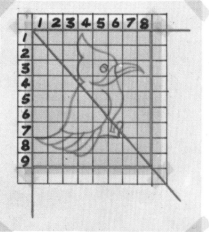

3. Place another, larger sheet of tracing paper on top of the pattern. Fix it in place with tape. Trace two sides of the rectangle and draw a diagonal through the two corners, as shown.

4

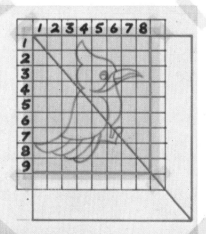

4. Decide how big you want your new pattern to be and draw a rectangle to that size.
Make sure the lines meet at the diagonal, as in the picture above.

5

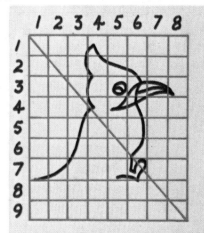

5. Divide your new, larger rectangle into the same number of squares as the first rectangle.
Carefully copy the pattern, square by square.

Triangle pop-up

Surprise your friends with original pop-up cards. They are easy to make once you know the basic techniques. You will make them more successfully if you use the right kind of paper. Choose a good quality uncoated paper, such as cover paper, which you can buy in all sorts of colors from art supply stores.

This is a simple pop-up technique to try, using a triangular fold in the center crease of the card.
Once you have made the airplane card, you will be able to use it as a basis for many other ideas – for a start, the airplane trail could be turned into the rays of a Christmas star or a Spanish skirt.

7

7. Open out the paper and fold it back into the original card shape. Keep the center crease in place with the thumb and forefinger of your left hand and bend the card up slightly. Use your right hand to ease the triangular pop-up shape into position.

8

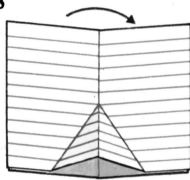

8. Close the card carefully, helping the pop-up outwards if necessary. Continue opening and closing the card until the pop-up works smoothly.

Airplane card

▶ You will need:
☐ White cover paper measuring 20cm x 30cm
☐ Pencil
☐ Coins or a pair of compasses
☐ Colored felt-tipped pens
☐ Paints

1. Fold the card in half twice to make a card shape 10cm x 15cm and make the pop-up shape described at the top of the opposite page. Draw cloud shapes, in pencil, across the card, using coins and a glass or a pair of compasses to make the arcs.
2. Paint the sky and pop-up triangle blue.

1
fold one

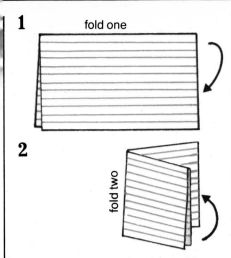

2
fold two

It is a good idea to practice making creases on ordinary lined paper before you start using more expensive papers.

1. Fold a piece of paper in half.
2. Fold it in half again.

3   4
fold three

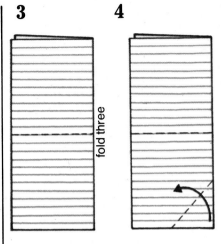

3. Open out the paper. Refold it in half along the long edge and press down the crease.
4. Fold over the bottom right-hand corner of the card, from halfway up the central crease to halfway along the lower edge.

5   6

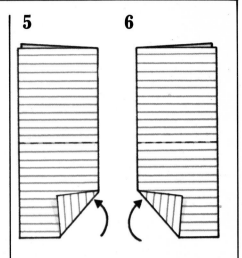

5. Press the fold sharply to make a crease.
6. Turn the card over and fold the crease the other way. Fold the corner several times in both directions to make the crease workable.

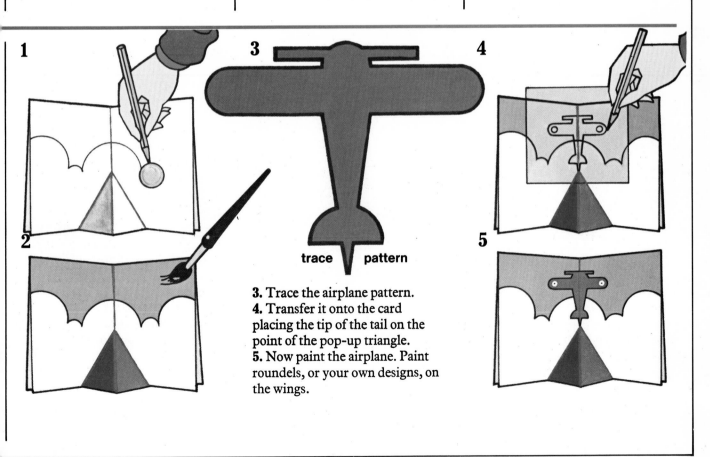

1
2
3
trace   pattern
4
5

3. Trace the airplane pattern.
4. Transfer it onto the card placing the tip of the tail on the point of the pop-up triangle.
5. Now paint the airplane. Paint roundels, or your own designs, on the wings.

Cut-out pop-up

Elephant card

▶ You will need:
- [ ] Pale gray cover paper measuring 20cm x 30cm
- [ ] Pencil and paints
- [ ] Black felt-tipped pen
- [ ] Scissors
- [ ] Pair of compasses or a cup
- [ ] Ruler
- [ ] Scrap of white paper
- [ ] Glue

1. Fold the gray paper in half.
2. Fold it in half again to make a card shape 10cm x 15cm.
3. Open out the paper and refold it down the long edge.
Trace the elephant face, but not the tusks, and transfer it onto the lower edge of the card. Place the top edge of the pattern along the first foldline.
4. Cut out the face through both layers of paper.

5   **6**

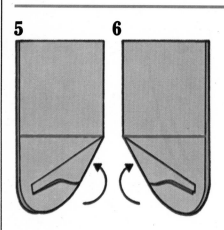

5. Fold the elephant's face along the dotted line to make a crease.
6. Turn the card over and fold the crease the other way.

7

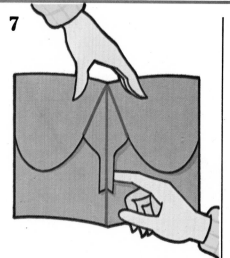

7. Refold the card along the first foldline. Hold down the ears with the thumb and forefinger of your left hand and use your right hand to ease the face into a pop-up position. Work the card open and shut to get the pop-up working smoothly.

8

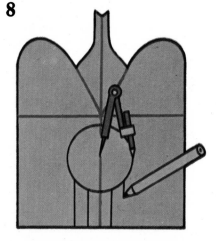

8. Draw a circle for the body on the inside of the card using the compasses with a 5cm radius, or a cup. Add two legs, each 2·5cm wide and 2·5cm apart.

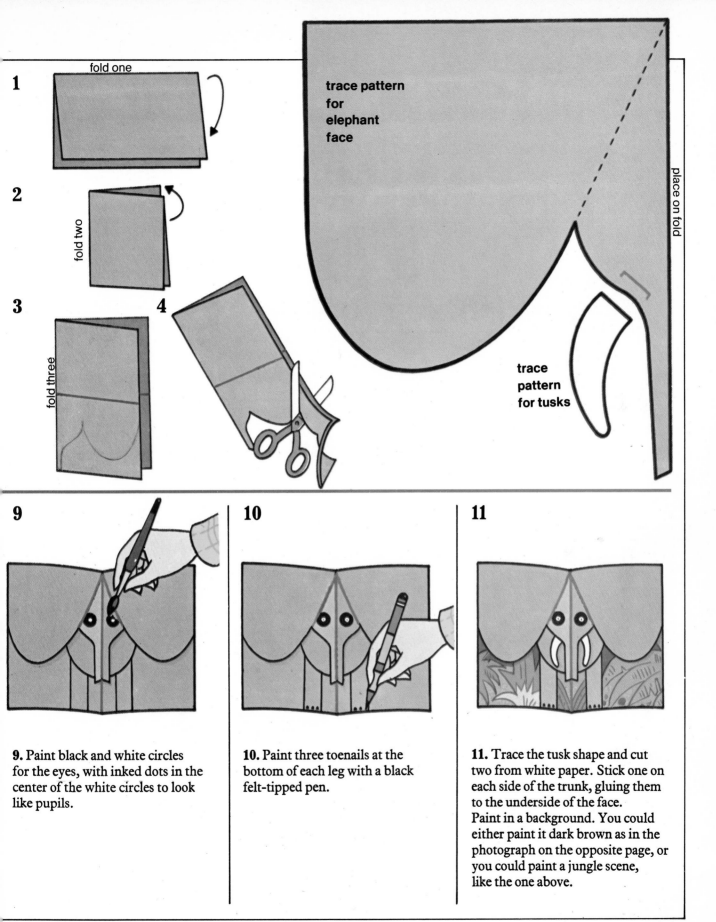

1 fold one

2 fold two

3 fold three

4

trace pattern
for
elephant
face

place on fold

trace
pattern
for tusks

9. Paint black and white circles for the eyes, with inked dots in the center of the white circles to look like pupils.

10. Paint three toenails at the bottom of each leg with a black felt-tipped pen.

11. Trace the tusk shape and cut two from white paper. Stick one on each side of the trunk, gluing them to the underside of the face.
Paint in a background. You could either paint it dark brown as in the photograph on the opposite page, or you could paint a jungle scene, like the one above.

Diamond pop-up

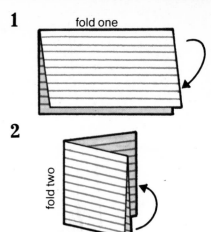

2

fold two

Now try this technique of cutting a slit across a folded piece of paper and making a talking mouth or a quacking beak.
Again it is a good idea to practice first on some lined paper.

1. Fold a piece of paper in half.
2. Fold it in half again.

8

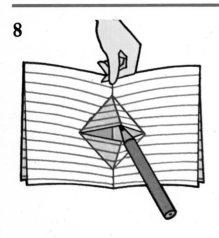

8. Hold down the center crease with your left hand and lift the top pop-up fold with a pencil. Turn the card upside-down and do the same to the other half of the pop-up. Carefully shut the card, if necessary helping the pop-ups outwards and keeping the top and bottom creases folding with the center fold of the card.

9

9. Open and shut the card several times to get the pop-up working smoothly. The movement should suggest an idea for a picture. Does it remind you of a fish's mouth or the winking eye of a frog, like the one in this picture? If it reminds you of a duck's beak, you could draw a face to match and write *Quack!* inside the beak.

1

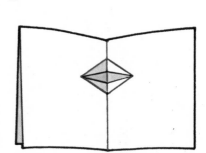

Bird card

▶ You will need:
☐ White cover paper measuring 20cm x 30cm
☐ Scissors
☐ Paints or colored felt-tipped pens
☐ Small coins and a cup

1. Follow steps 1–8 of 'Try it first' to make the bird's beak.

3   **4**

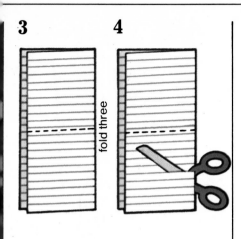

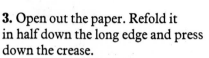

5

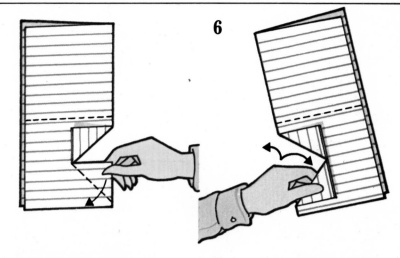

6

3. Open out the paper. Refold it in half down the long edge and press down the crease.

4. Make a slit, 4cm long, through the fold, about 20cm down from the top edge of the paper.

5. Fold back the edges of the slit to make two right-angled triangles.
6. Turn the paper over and fold these triangles the other way. Fold the triangles once or twice in both directions to emphasize the creases.
7. Open out the paper and fold it back into the original card shape, with the slit half facing you.

7

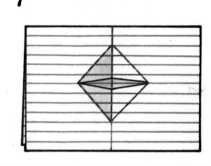

2

3

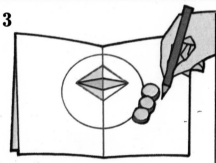

4

2. Make the body shape by drawing round a cup in a suitable position on the card.

3. Draw round three small coins, placed in a row, to make the tail. Color the whole body shape in.

4. Color the beak yellow and draw on two yellow feet. Draw on the wing shapes with a black felt-tipped pen. Finally draw in the eyes and add black inked spots for the pupils.

If you prefer, you could cut all the features out of colored gummed labels and stick them in position.

Window panels

Decorative cut-out window panels can change the look of your room, or help create a gay atmosphere for special occasions.

Tissue paper is ideal for making window panels. It cuts easily, it creases crisply but will iron out smoothly once the design is complete. It is available in a wide range of colors, and, most important, will not keep out the light.

As well as using cut-outs for window panels, you can use them to decorate greeting cards.

5

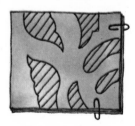

6

5. On the top fold, copy the design above lightly in pencil.
6. Fix together the open edges with paper clips. This will stop the folded layers from slipping while you cut.
Shade in the area you are going to cut.

Before you make the panels in tissue paper, try making them first with plain paper.
Experiment with patterns of your own, or try out some of the designs shown in the photograph on the opposite page.

▶ You will need:
☐ Several sheets of plain paper or tissue paper
☐ Scissors
☐ Pencil
☐ Rubber cement
☐ Paper clips
☐ Iron

1

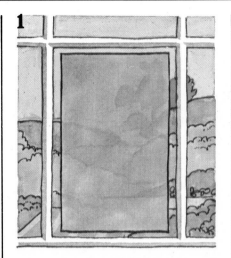

1. Measure a pane in your window. Decide how many panes you want to decorate and cut a piece of paper for each one. Make each piece about 2cm smaller all round than the size of the panes.

2
3
4

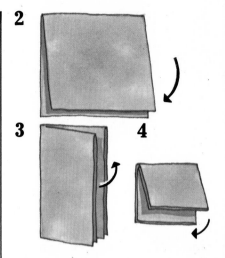

2. Fold one of the sheets of paper firmly in half crosswise.
3. Fold it in half again.
4. Then fold it in half once more.

7

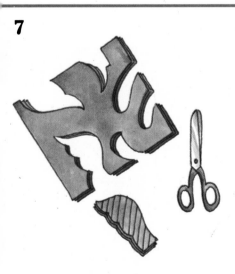

7. Following the lines of the shaded area, cut through all the layers of paper with a pair of sharp pointed scissors.
8. Open out the paper. Press out the folds with a warm iron.

8

9

9. Put little dabs of rubber cement at the four corners of the panel and stick it to the pane. When you want to take off the panels roll the glue off with your fingers.

13

Flying angels and birds

These are two more fold and cut ideas to try, using different folds. Once you have mastered the technique, you could make up your own patterns; or you could try using the other patterns for fold and cut on pages 44 and 45.

You could use these cut-outs to make mobiles or Christmas decorations, or use them as doilies.

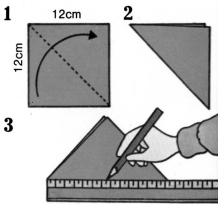

Flying birds

1. Cut a piece of paper into a square 12cm x 12cm.

2. Fold it in half along the diagonal to make a triangle.

3. Measure the long edge of the triangle and mark the center point.

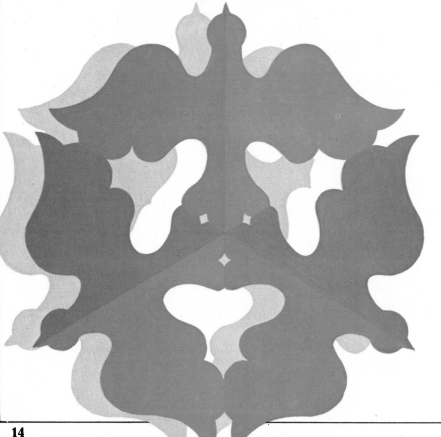

1

12cm

12cm

2

Flying angel

▶ You will need:
- [ ] Several sheets of thin paper
- [ ] Scissors
- [ ] Tracing paper
- [ ] Pencil

1. Cut a sheet of paper into a square 12cm x 12cm.
2. Fold it in half.
3. Trace the angel shape.

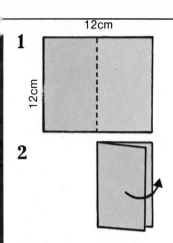

3

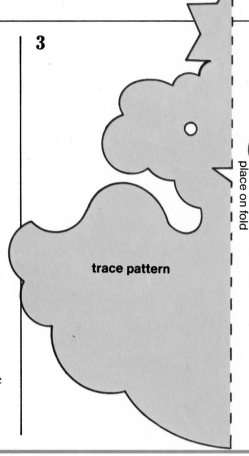

trace pattern

place on fold

4

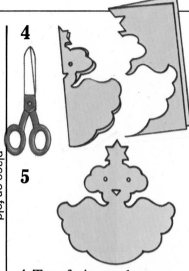

5

4. Transfer it onto the paper, placing the straight line along the fold. Cut it out.
5. Open out the paper and your angel should look like the one in this picture. If you wanted, you could make a border of angels. See page 45 for instructions on how to do this.

4

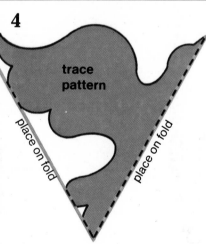

trace pattern

place on fold

place on fold

4. Trace just the blue dotted V-shape from the pattern above.

5

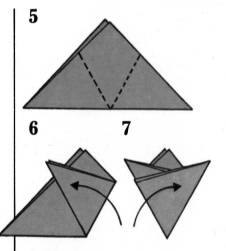

6   **7**

5. Transfer it onto the paper, placing the tip on the center point of the long edge.
6. Fold one point along one of the lines you have just traced.
7. Then fold the other point along the other line.

8

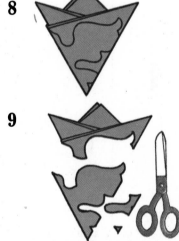

9

8. Trace the bird shape and transfer it onto the top fold, placing the dotted edges of the shape exactly onto the folds of the paper.
9. Cut out the bird shape and then open the paper out. Be careful not to cut the parts of the shape that are on the fold.

Doily dolls

The quaint little angels in the picture at the bottom of the opposite page are made with doilies. Doilies are lacy paper mats sold for putting under cakes. But if you haven't got a doily, you can make your own.

Use angels and dancing girls for decorating a Christmas tree or hanging from a mobile or a lamp.

Start by experimenting with paper patterns for a do-it-yourself doily to make a skirt for a dancing girl.

▶ You will need:
☐ Sheet of lightweight pink paper 15cm x 15cm
☐ Scissors
☐ Pencil, crayons or felt-tipped pens
☐ Sewing thread
☐ Stiff white paper

1. Cut pink paper 15cm x 15cm.
2. Fold the piece of paper in half diagonally.
3. Fold it in half again.
4. Fold it in half once again.
5. Fold it in half again.
Make each crease as sharp as possible.

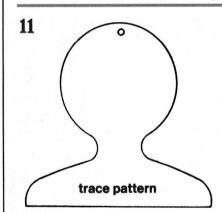

11. Trace the head shape shown above and transfer it onto stiff white paper. Cut it out.

Draw a face and hair on it in colors of your own choice.
Make a hole in the head and push through the sewing thread. Knot the ends together.

trace pattern

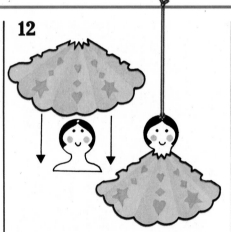

12. Push the skirt down over the head, so that two folds sit on the 'shoulders' like a dress on a hanger. If by any chance the skirt won't go over, make a small slit on either side. Now you can make lots more dancing girls, with every skirt a different color.

Golden-haired angels

▶ You will need:
☐ Bought or home-made doilies
☐ Scraps of pink, stiff white paper
☐ Scraps of tinsel ribbon and tinsel braid
☐ Gold thread
☐ Scissors, white glue, pencil, felt-tipped pen

Cut out the head shape as in step 11.
Make a doily following steps 1–10, or pleat a bought doily and cut out the center.
Put the skirt over the head.
Glue scraps of tinsel braid round the neck to make a ruff.
Draw dots for eyes with the pen and glue on pink circles for cheeks.
Fray the tinsel ribbon a bit and glue it on to make hair.
Loop the gold thread through a hole in the angel's head.

1

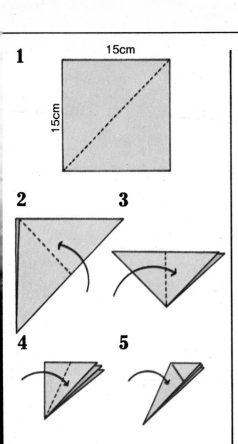

15cm

15cm

2   **3**

4   **5**

6   **7**

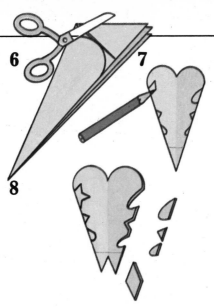

8

6. Draw a curve as shown and cut along the line you have drawn.
7. Open up one fold. Mark a line 1·5cm down from the point. Draw some shapes on the sides of the triangle between the mark and the curved edge.
8. Cut out the shapes and the tip of the triangle with a V-shaped snip.

9

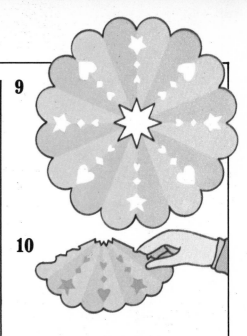

10

9. Open up the round paper cut-out.
10. Re-pleat the folds all the way round, so that the cut-out folds stick out and the plain folds go in.

It is worth buying the firmest tissue you can find. The results will be better and longer lasting. Tissue paper colors fade over time and this will happen more quickly if the paper is exposed to sunlight. Always arrange tissue paper flowers well away from the window. Take care never to get tissue paper wet. Even a few spots of water will make the dye run and spoil the paper.

Save all the scraps you'll have left over from making paper flowers. You can use them for making paper beads, described on pages 22 and 23, or twisted paper jewelry, described on pages 24 to 27.

The basic folds for making paper flowers are the same as those for making the doilies described on the previous page. The main difference is in the way you cut the paper.

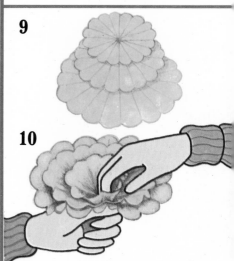

Pretty paper peonies

Tissue paper versions of flowers are very decorative and have the delicate appearance of real ones. Peonies are large striking flowers that look particularly life-like made in tissue paper. The dark red varieties are the most common, but peonies can also be two-toned in shades of white and gold, pink and cream or pale and deep pink.

9. Open out the cones and put them on top of one another in order of size, with the smallest one on the top.
10. Put your right hand in the center of the smallest layer of petals and gather the petals together with your left hand.

1

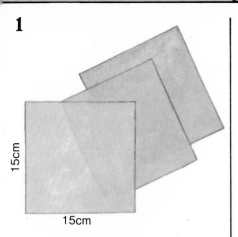

15cm

15cm

▶ You will need:
☐ Tissue paper or thin paper
☐ Scissors
☐ Pencil
☐ Tape

1. Cut three squares of tissue paper 15cm x 15cm.

2 **3**

4 **5**

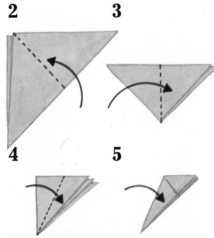

2. Fold each square in half diagonally.
3. Then fold each one in half again.
4. Fold each one in half yet again.
5. Fold each one in half once more to make a cone.
Make each crease as sharp as possible.

6

7

8

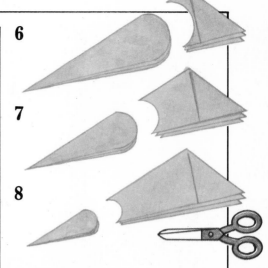

6. Hold the point of the first cone tightly with your left hand and cut a curve.
7. Hold the point of the second cone and cut a curve at a slightly lower place than the curve on the first cone.
8. Hold the point of the third cone and cut a curve at an even lower place.

11

12

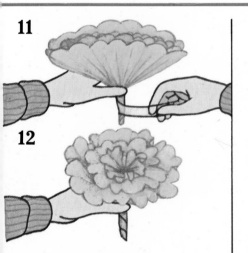

11. Twist the bottom point and fix it with tape.
12. Separate the petals out into a flower shape.

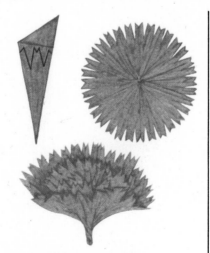

Now try different ways of cutting the petals to see what flower shapes they produce. First fold a few squares following steps 1–5 shown above.

If you cut lots of sharp little points the flower will look like a carnation or a cornflower.

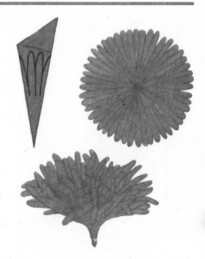

If you cut lots of long ribbony petals the flower will look like a chrysanthemum or a daisy.

Two pretty peonies

▶ You will need:
- ☐ 2 sheets of tissue paper about 50cm x 74cm, each in a different shade such as pale and deep pink, or white and gold
- ☐ 15cm of sturdy (1·5mm) wire
- ☐ Very fine flexible wire, or green plastic-covered wire
- ☐ Green crêpe paper
- ☐ White glue

1. Divide each sheet of tissue into six equal squares by folding the paper in half lengthwise and then into three crosswise. Cut the tissue along the foldlines.
For each flower you will need three squares of one shade, for the center petals, and three squares of the other shade, for the outer petals.

1

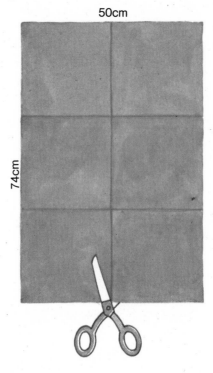

50cm

74cm

2

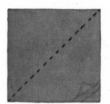

2. Put the three squares of one color on top of one another and the three squares of the other color on top of one another.

---

10   **11**

12   **13**

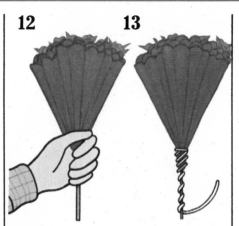

14

10. Straighten the sturdy wire. Bend one end of the wire over to prevent the petals from falling off.
11. Push the other end of the wire down through the center of all six layers of petals.

12. Slide the petals up to the wire hook and fold them into an umbrella shape around it. Hold them in place until the glue begins to harden.
13. Bind the base of the flower tightly with very fine wire or green plastic-covered wire, and then wrap it round the length of the stem.

14. To shape the flower, gently separate the three outer petals and turn them downwards. Separate the inner petals and turn them upwards.

3   **4**

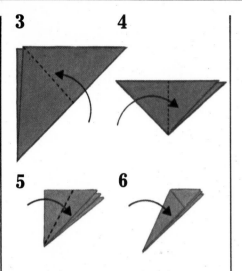

5   **6**

3. Taking each set of squares in turn, fold the paper in half.
4. Then fold it in half again.
5. Fold it in half yet again.
6. Fold the triangle into a cone shape.

7   **8**

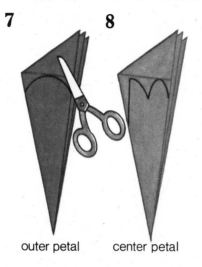

outer petal   center petal

7. Draw the shape of the outer petals on one of the cones. Cut the shape out.
8. Draw the shape of the center petals on the other cone. Cut the shape out.

9

9. Spread out the petals but do not flatten them.
Dab a spot of glue onto the center of each petal and place the three center petals on top of the three outer petals. Take care to keep the creases in.

---

15   **16**

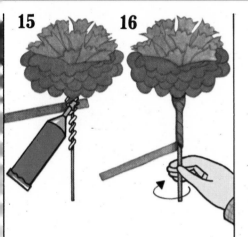

15. Wrap a strip of green crêpe paper about 2·5cm wide very tightly around the base of the flower; dab glue on the end of the strip to hold it in position.
16. Turning the wire, wrap the paper strip tightly around the length of the stem in a bandaging movement.

17

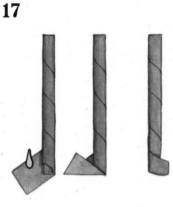

17. Fold the paper neatly around the base of the stem and fix it with another dab of glue.

18. The photograph above shows the final flower head.

Now you can make other sorts of flowers in colored tissue paper based on the shapes you practiced in 'Try it first'.

Bead necklaces

Paper beads of assorted shapes and sizes look very striking strung together to make a necklace. You can use almost any kind of paper to make beads, so this is a good way to use up paper scraps left over from other projects.

▶ You will need:
- ☐ Paper scraps
- ☐ White glue
- ☐ Scissors
- ☐ Used matchsticks
- ☐ Needle and thread
- ☐ Ruler (for oblong beads)
- ☐ Knitting needle
- ☐ Clear varnish or acrylic spray (optional)
- ☐ Paints

Oblong beads

You can use patterned or plain paper, heavy or thin. If you want to decorate the beads it is best to use white paper. Try a mixture of shapes and sizes on each string of beads, but keep to the same sort of paper throughout a necklace; thin papers make delicate beads that will look lost beside chunky beads made from thicker papers.

1. Using a ruler, draw and cut out a number of strips of different widths and lengths.
Roll strips 1cm x 30cm to make fat beads. Roll strips 2cm x 15cm to make broader beads.
2. For tapered beads, use a pencil to mark out a piece of paper in ruler widths. Join these pencil lines from top to bottom diagonally, to make long thin triangles. Cut them out.

1

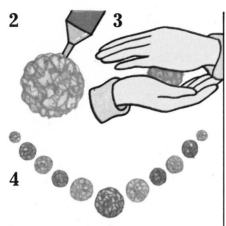

12cm

9cm

7cm

Round beads

These look their best made in tissue paper or other thin brightly colored types of paper.

1. Decide how many beads you want to put on your necklace and cut out a paper circle for each one. For the smallest back beads, the circles should be about 7cm across, for the medium-sized beads about 9cm across and for the largest front beads about 10–12cm across.

2 **3**

4

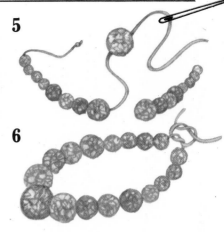

2. Scrunch up each circle into a ball shape. Squeeze glue between the cracks and pinch the beads until the glue is tacky.
3. Roll each ball between your palms and then leave them to dry completely.
4. Arrange the balls in order of size as the picture shows.

5

6

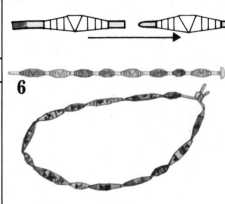

5. Cut a piece of thread long enough to slip over your head. Add an extra 13cm for threading the needle and finishing off. Thread the needle and make a double knot at one end. Take the needle through each of the beads in turn.
6. To finish off, tie a double knot to join the ends of the thread together, cutting off any that is left over.

1

1cm   2cm

2

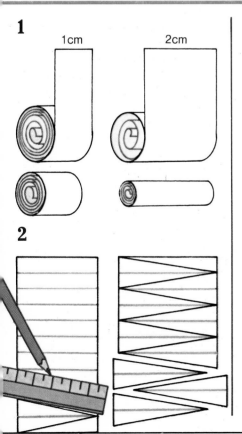

3

4

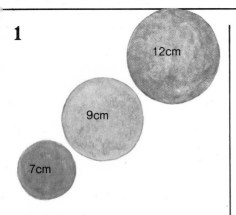

3. Dab glue on the wrong side of one end of a strip and roll it tightly and evenly towards you onto a used matchstick.
4. When about 3cm of the paper is left unwound, dab glue on the end of the strip.
Continue rolling the paper so that the glued end is rolled up. Hold the roll for a few seconds until the glue begins to dry.

5

6

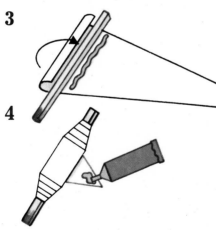

5. Carefully slip the bead off the matchstick and onto a thin knitting needle. Leave it for half an hour to dry.
6. When the beads are dry, you can paint designs on them and paint them all over with varnish. Thread them in the same way you thread the round beads (see steps 5–6).

Stones and strings

Save torn, creased and odd-shaped pieces of tissue paper to make bright jewels.

There are only two basic jewel shapes – stones and strings – but they can be used in all sorts of ways. Make simple pictures by sticking the jewels onto cardboard. Cover old boxes and tins with tissue paper and use twisted tissue jewels as decoration. Cut shapes in cardboard and stick tissue jewels on both sides. Pierce the shapes and thread them with wool yarn. Then you can use them for Christmas decorations.

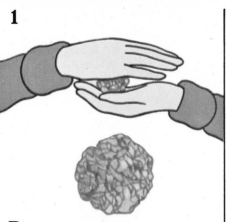

Paper stones

▶ You will need:
Some tissue paper scraps, white glue and a pair of scissors

1. Screw up some tissue paper into a ball and roll it between your palms. With a bit of practice you will be able to judge how much tissue you need for different-sized stones.

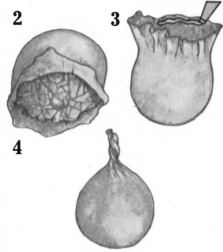

2. Wrap the ball tightly in a piece of tissue just large enough to cover it.
3. Cover the ball with another, larger piece of tissue. Spread a little glue inside the tissue neck.
4. Tightly twist the neck.

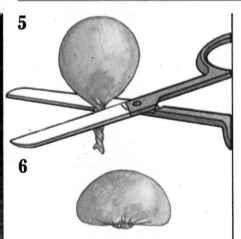

5. When the glue has dried, snip off the neck with a pair of sharp scissors.
6. Press the ball into the palm of your hand to give it a domed top and a flattened base. This will make it easier to mount.

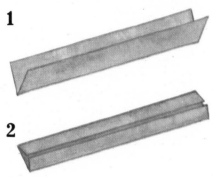

Paper strings

▶ You will need:
Some long, thin tissue scraps, a pencil and ruler and a pair of scissors

1. Cut a tissue strip 3cm x 23cm. Fold it in half to make a crease and then unfold it.
2. Fold the long edges towards the central crease.

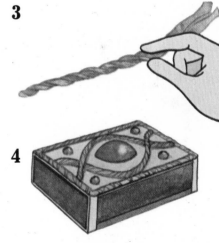

3. Wet both thumbs and forefingers. Carefully twist the tissue strip into a string. Work slowly from one end to the other, always twisting in the same direction.
4. Cover an old box with your stones and strings. Dab glue where you want to put them and press them in position.

Bird brooch and bangle

Twisted tissue jewelry would make a good present for an older sister or friend. As well as creating a brooch and a bangle like the ones in the pictures, you could also try a ring, pendant or some earrings.

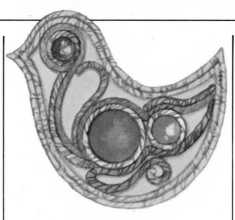

Bird brooch

▶ You will need:
- ☐ Cardboard
- ☐ Tracing paper and pencil
- ☐ Tissue paper in various colors
- ☐ Glue or paper paste
- ☐ Scissors
- ☐ Tweezers
- ☐ Safety pin
- ☐ Small paper fastener
- ☐ Clear varnish or acrylic spray
- ☐ Tape

trace pattern

1. Trace the bird shape above and transfer it onto a piece of cardboard. Cut it out.
2. Draw round the cardboard shape onto a piece of tissue paper. Roughly cut out the tissue bird shape adding about 1cm all round, and put it aside for the moment.

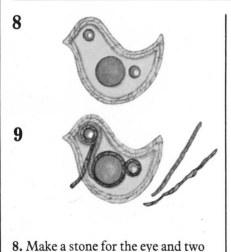

8. Make a stone for the eye and two others for the body. Put glue on the backs and press them into position.
9. Make several strings in different colors. Dab glue in the places where you want to put the strings and then press the strings in place, using tweezers to help you position them. When the brooch is dry, lightly apply a coat of clear varnish.

Bangle

▶ You will need:
- ☐ Cardboard
- ☐ Tissue paper in various colors
- ☐ Tape measure
- ☐ Ruler
- ☐ Pencil
- ☐ Paper clips
- ☐ Scissors
- ☐ Pair of tweezers
- ☐ Glue or paper paste
- ☐ Clear varnish

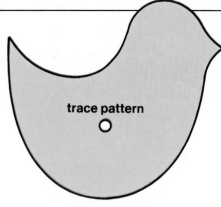

cover   cardboard   lining

1. Cut cardboard 5cm wide and long enough to fit round your hand at the knuckle, adding an extra 1cm to the length. Cut another piece of tissue paper the same size as the cardboard – this will be the lining.

1

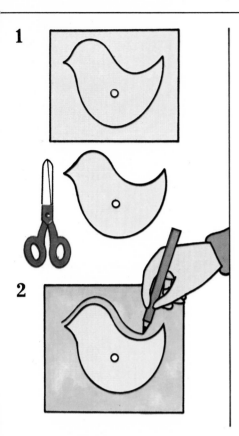

2

3

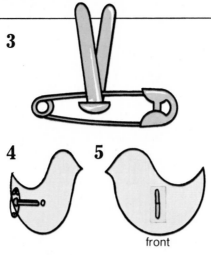

4 **5**

front

3. Put the closed safety pin over one of the prongs of the paper fastener.

4. Pierce a hole in the center of the bird with the point of your scissors. Push the paper fastener through the hole from the wrong side of the bird.

5. Open out the paper fastener on the right side of the bird and fix it in place with tape.

6

7

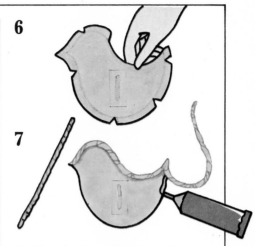

6. Glue the tissue bird onto the cardboard one, wrapping it round the edges. Don't worry if there are one or two wrinkles.

7. Make two strings in the same color tissue as the bird's body. Glue round the edge of the bird and press the strings in place along the glueline.

2

3

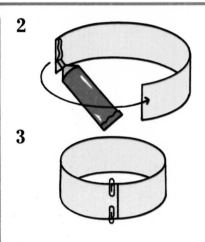

2. Mark the overlap on the cardboard and cover it with glue. Make the strip into a ring, overlapping the glued end by 1cm.

3. Put paper clips at the top and bottom of the overlap. This will hold the cardboard in a circular shape while it dries.

4

5

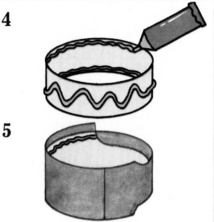

4. When the bangle is dry, cover it with tissue paper. Cover the outside of the bangle with glue and spread a little glue on the inside top and bottom edges.

5. Press the tissue into position round the bangle, folding 6mm over onto the top and bottom inside edges.

6

7

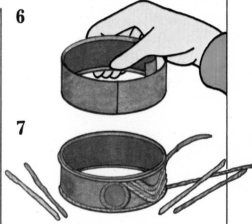

6. To line the bangle, spread glue on the inside of the bangle and press the tissue lining in place.

7. Make strings and stones for the bangle. Remember to stick the stones on first.

When the bangle is dry, coat it lightly with varnish or acrylic spray.

How to make funny faces

Funny face masks like these are as much fun to make as to wear, either to a costume party or to disguise yourself from your family and friends. But don't forget that younger children are easily frightened by a sudden and, to them, terrifying change in a once-familiar face!

The three masks on the facing page are all made from large brown paper bags (the kind that have side gussets) with features of paper or cotton wool added on. If you cannot get hold of brown paper bags from the supermarket, you can use white paper bags or shopping bags. *Never* use *any* kind of plastic bag for making a mask – a plastic bag, placed even lightly over the head, can all too easily lead to suffocation.

▶ You will need:
- ☐ Large paper bags with gussets
- ☐ Black felt-tipped pen
- ☐ Poster paints or crayons
- ☐ Colored paper or gummed labels for smaller features
- ☐ Scissors
- ☐ Colored chalk or a soft pencil
- ☐ Drinking glass, dinner plate and coins or a pair of compasses
- ☐ Glue or paper paste
- ☐ Tape or staples

1

1. Before making any of these masks, first pull the paper bag over your head until it sits comfortably on your shoulders.

2

2. Ask a friend to press the bag gently against your face and to mark your eyes, nose and mouth lightly in chalk or soft pencil.

3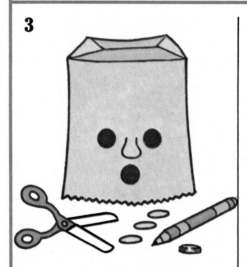

3. Then remove the bag and cut out a small, pear-shaped flap for your nose, and three small circles about 2cm in diameter for your eyes and mouth. You can draw round a coin to make perfect circles.

4

4. Practice making different expressions. Use the black felt-tipped pen to draw mean little piggy eyes and a pair of eyebrows. Then put more and more lines round the eyes until they look very big. Try different shapes for mouths too.

1

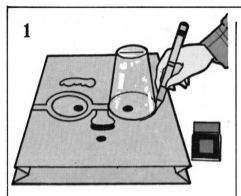

Grandpa mask

▶ You will need:
Stiff paper, red tissue paper, and cotton wool, as well as the materials on page 28.

1. Cut out the eye and mouth holes and cut the nose-flap.
Use a glass or a pair of compasses to draw the spectacle frames.
Color them in with poster paint or crayon. Color in the eyebrows above the spectacles.

2

2. Trace the ear shape on the facing page and transfer it onto a piece of stiff paper. Cut out the shape and then draw round it to make another ear shape. Outline the edges of both ears with a black felt-tipped pen. Fold along the dotted line and glue the tabs. Stick the ears in place on either side of the bag.

3   **4**

5

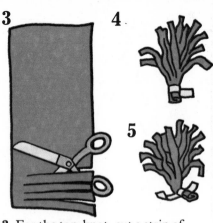

3. For the top-knot, cut a strip of red tissue paper 15cm x 30cm. Cut it into thin strands just shorter than the width of the paper.
4. Bunch the strands together at the uncut edge and tape them together.
5. Bend the taped end and fix it to the center of the paper bag base with tape.

1

Soldier boy mask

▶ You will need:
Yellow tissue paper, green, yellow and red paper as well as the materials on page 28.

1. Cut out the eye and mouth holes and cut the nose-flap.
Color the base and bottom quarter of the bag all over with black poster paint or crayon.
Stick a band of green paper along the edge of the bag.

2   **3**

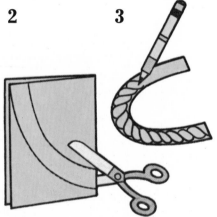

2. To make the chin-strap, cut a piece of yellow paper the size of the space between the black 'hat' and the green band. Fold it in half and draw two parallel curved lines about 2cm apart. Cut along the lines and unfold the paper.
3. Draw on the 'rope' pattern with a black felt-tipped pen.

4   **5**

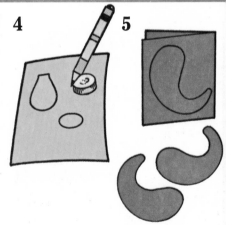

4. From the yellow scraps cut a pear-shaped piece to cover the nose-flap and two yellow discs for the chin-strap buttons (you can use a large coin or a pair of compasses to draw the discs).
5. Trace the moustache shape shown at the top of the facing page.
Transfer the shape onto red paper, folded as shown, to make both a right and a left moustache shape.

6

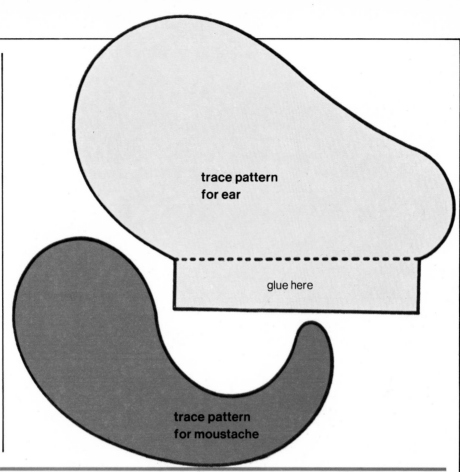

trace pattern
for ear

glue here

trace pattern
for moustache

6. Pull a flat piece of cotton wool into a beard that will cover the lower part of the mask from the nose downwards. Make a moustache from another small strip.
Stick the moustache and beard in place, shaping them further if necessary.

6

6. To make the epaulettes, cut two strips of yellow tissue paper about 15cm x 30cm as you did for Grandpa's red top-knot. Bunch them together at the uncut edge, then fix them firmly to the edges of the gussets with staples or tape. To finish the mask, stick on the chin-strap, then the buttons and nose-flap and finally the moustache.

1

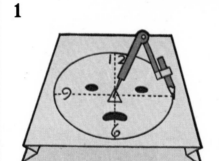

Alarm clock mask

1. Cut out the eye and mouth holes and cut the nose-flap.
Lay the bag flat. With the point of a pair of compasses at the center of the nose-flap draw a circle that almost touches the sides of the bag. Divide the circle in quarters and mark in 12, 3, 6 and 9 o'clock in pencil. Space the other numbers evenly in between.

2   **3**

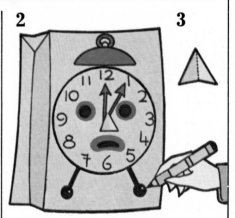

2. Draw the alarm bell and the clock feet. Draw circles round the eye holes and add clock hands.
Color over all the pencil outlines.
3. Cut out a triangle of colored paper to stick on the nose-flap.

Boxes and bows

There are many colorful papers you can use for wrapping presents. Or you can use crêpe paper, tissue paper or even plain white or brown paper. Crêpe paper stretches, so you can pull it to fit the shape of your parcel very neatly. Tissue paper is thin and fragile, but if you use several sheets together you will find it easier to work with. Try using sheets of different colors together. If you want a shiny effect, cover your wrapping paper with cellophane.

Practice wrapping a box with scrap paper, or newspaper, before you use a specially bought wrapping paper.

▶ You will need:
Scrap paper, a pair of scissors and some double-coated tape.

Boxes

1. Cut a piece of paper longer than your box and wide enough to fit around it. Center the paper under the box and wrap it around the box.
2. Trim the paper so that it extends over both ends of the box by a little more than half the depth of the box.
3. Turn under the overlap and fix it with double-coated tape.
4. Fold in the sides at both ends.

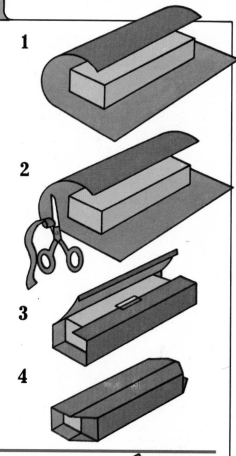

5. Turn down the top flap.
6. Turn up the bottom flap and fix it to the top flap with double-coated tape.

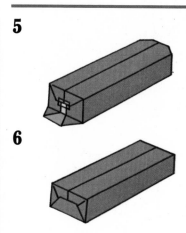

Tubes

1. Cut a piece of paper slightly longer than your tube and wide enough to wrap it around several times. Wrap the paper around the tube.
2. Turn under the long edge and fix it with double-coated tape.

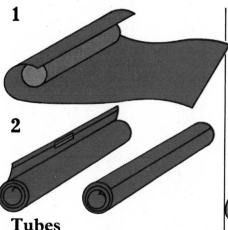

3. Tie the ends with ribbons, so that the tube looks like a cracker.
4. If you want to make fringes on the ends, snip the edges of the paper up to the ribbons.

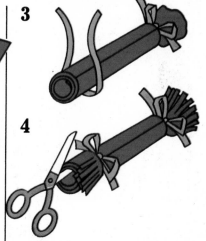

Swirl bow

Once you have made a swirl bow in one size, you can experiment with making it larger or smaller, and adding more petals.

▶ You will need:
Some narrow self-stick gift wrapping ribbon in two colors, and a pair of scissors

1

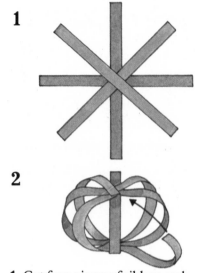

1. Cut four pieces of ribbon each 28cm long – two in one color, two in the other color. Moisten the center of each one and stick them together in a criss-cross pattern in the color sequence shown.
2. Stick the ends of each piece of ribbon to make a ball shape.

3

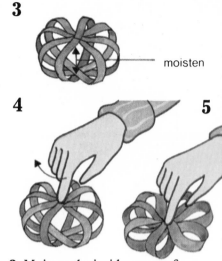

moisten

3. Moisten the inside center of the criss-cross.
4. Twist the top of the ball shape a quarter turn to the right.
5. Press it firmly to the bottom.

3

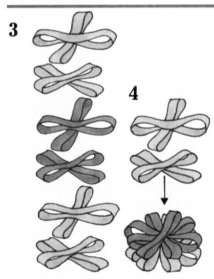

3. Make five more pairs in the same way so that you have six pairs in all. Follow the color sequence shown above.
4. Moisten the center of each pair of ribbons and press each bow in turn onto the one below. Fix each bow diagonally to the one below.

5

6

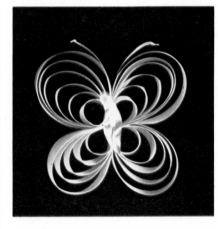

5. Cut a piece of ribbon about 12cm long and make it into a circle. Stick it to the center of the bow.
6. With a sharp scissors, snip two slashes from opposite directions into the outer edge of the loop.

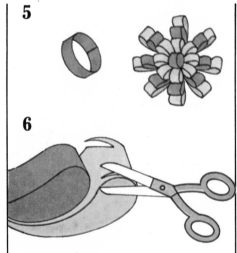

Butterfly bow

The steps show you how to make a great big butterfly with a wing span of about 25cm.

▶ You will need:
Some narrow self-stick gift wrapping ribbon in one color, a pair of scissors and a paper clip.

6

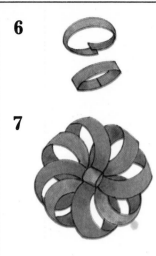

7

6. Cut a piece of ribbon 8cm long. Make it into a loop, stick the ends together, and flatten it.
7. Stick the loop to the center of the bow to cover all the ends.

Sunburst bow

This bow looks particularly effective if you make each circle of loops in a different color.

▶ You will need:
Some narrow self-stick gift wrapping ribbon in two colors, and a pair of scissors

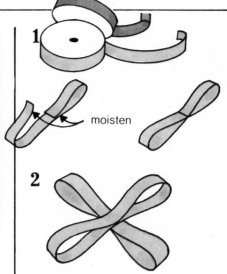

moisten

1. Cut twelve strips of ribbon each 20cm long – eight in one color, and four in the other color. Moisten both ends of one piece of ribbon and press them to the center to make a bow.
2. Join another piece in the same way and stick it crosswise to the bow you have just made.

---

1. First make the upper wings. Cut six strips of ribbon – one each of 10cm, 15cm, 20cm, 25cm, 30cm and 35cm.
2. Stick the ends of each strip together to make a ring.
3. Put the rings one inside the other, with the joins all in one place. Moisten them at the joins and press them together to stick them.
4. Pinch them at the base of the wing to make an oval shape. Make another six-ring wing in the same way.
5. Make the lower wings in the same way, but with only five smaller rings.
6. Moisten the four wings at the joins and stick them together at the center. Use a paper clip to hold them together if it helps.

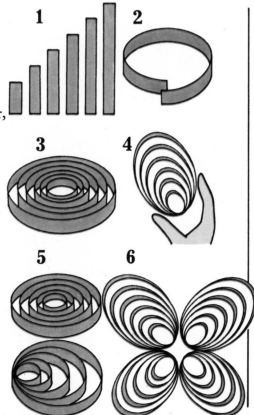

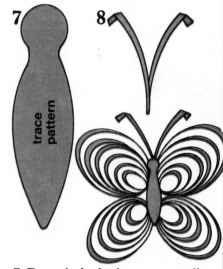

trace pattern

7. Draw the body shape on a small piece of ribbon and cut it out. Stick the body to the wings.
8. Cut a piece of ribbon 8cm long. for the antennae. Split it in half to make two thinner pieces. Pinch two ends between your fingers and stick the other ends between the upper wings.

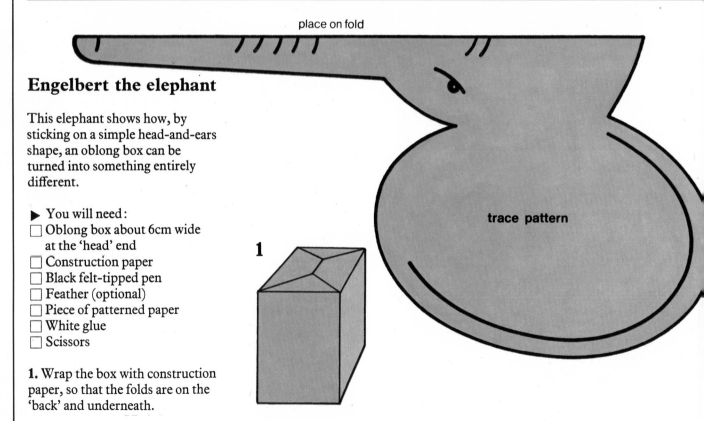

place on fold

Engelbert the elephant

This elephant shows how, by sticking on a simple head-and-ears shape, an oblong box can be turned into something entirely different.

▶ You will need:
☐ Oblong box about 6cm wide at the 'head' end
☐ Construction paper
☐ Black felt-tipped pen
☐ Feather (optional)
☐ Piece of patterned paper
☐ White glue
☐ Scissors

1. Wrap the box with construction paper, so that the folds are on the 'back' and underneath.

trace pattern

Animal boxes

It's easy to turn boxes and tubes into paper sculpture once you have learned how to gift wrap a parcel (see page 32). Boxes with deep lids are best because they do not make a ridge under the wrapping paper. Large matchboxes are good too.

Think where you are going to fold the ends of the paper: if you want to have a face at the end of the box, you will want to make the folds at the top and bottom of the box, or on the sides.

See how many ways you can turn an ordinary oblong box into a cat or a dog, a suitcase or a high-rise building. You can glue on paper shapes or draw the details.

In a way you are drawing six pictures: a picture of the sides, the face, the tail, the back and the underneath. They should all join up so that the whole box looks like a complete, three-dimensional suitcase or animal or whatever you have in mind.

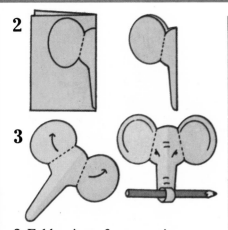

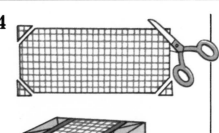
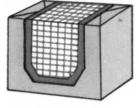

2. Fold a piece of construction paper in half. Trace the elephant's head shape and transfer it onto the paper with the top edge on the fold line. Cut the shape out.
3. Open out the head and fold up the ears along the dotted lines. Draw in the face and outline the ears with felt-tipped pen. Roll the tip of the trunk around a pencil to make it curl.

4. Cut a rectangle of the patterned paper wide enough to cover the fold on the 'back' of the box and long enough to hang down the sides. Snip off the corners. You can make an under-blanket if you like with a piece of plain construction paper about 0·5cm larger all round.

5. Attach the head to the box with a paper tab of the same color. To finish off, glue a feather to the elephant's forehead.
6. If you don't have a feather, fold and cut a piece of paper into half a feather shape. Use scissors to snip a feathery fringe all round. Open it out.

Sheila the sheep

This introduces an intriguing technique – paper curling. Once you have made some woolly-looking ringlets for Sheila the sheep, you can curl up the ends of paper ribbons on presents. Or you could make bangs or even a funny wig with ringlets.

▶ You will need:
- ☐ Oblong box with lid
- ☐ White construction paper
- ☐ Black felt-tipped pen, black ink or paint
- ☐ Scissors
- ☐ White glue

1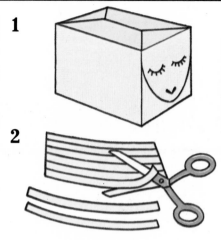

3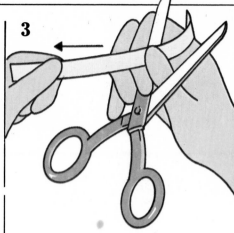

1. Wrap the box in white paper as in step 1 of 'Try it first.' Draw on a sheepish face with a black felt-tipped pen.
2. To make the woolly ringlets, cut strips of paper about 1·5cm wide and the length of the box.

3. To curl the ringlets, hold a strip in your left hand and tug the sharp side of the blade of the scissors quite firmly along the strip of paper, holding it against the blade with your right thumb.

Sammy the centipede

There are lots of interesting things you can turn tubes into—airplane bodies, caterpillars, high-speed trains. The only trouble is that long tubes, especially ones with ends, are much harder to find than square boxes.
The next few steps explain how to make your own tube.

▶ You will need:
- ☐ A sheet of construction paper, as long as the tube you want to make
- ☐ Some decorative paper
- ☐ Gold or yellow paint
- ☐ Pipe cleaner
- ☐ 2 paper stones for eyes
- ☐ Black felt-tipped pen
- ☐ Sheet of decorative paper as long as the tube
- ☐ White glue, tape

1 **2** **3**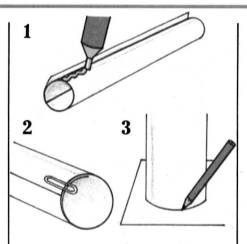

4 tags

5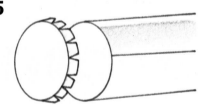

1. Roll up the sheet of construction paper into a tube with a diameter of about 4cm. Glue it together along the length.
2. You can pop a paper clip over the overlap to hold it down while it is drying.
3. Draw round the end of the tube onto a piece of paper.

4. Draw little tag shapes all round, about 0·5cm long. Cut out the tagged circle.
5. Bend all the tags up at right angles, put spots of glue on them and stick over one end of the tube. If you want to put a present inside, do it at this stage.
Repeat for the other end.
Paint gold or yellow if you want.

4

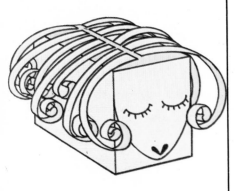

4. Glue the ringlets side by side along the top of the box, so that they hang over the sides. Make each curl a different length to give the sheep a shaggy look.

5

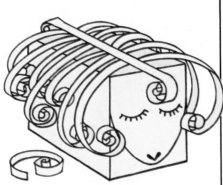

5. Cut a strip of paper twice the length of the box and curl it. Stick it down the middle of the box top, covering all the ends and the center fold as well as possible. Add a few curls to hang over the eyes and tail end.

6

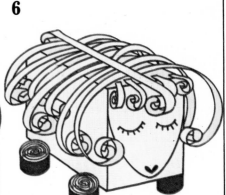

6. To make the feet, cut four strips of paper each 2cm wide and about 25cm long. Roll them into tubes about 3cm in diameter and glue down the ends.
Paint the outsides black.
Cover one end of each little tube generously with glue and stick them to the four corners of the bottom of the box. Don't touch them until they are really dry.

6

6. Cover the tube with a layer of decorative paper exactly the same length. Make sure it overlaps along the side and glue it along the join.

7

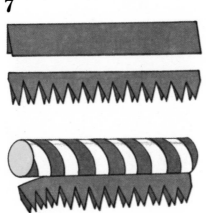

7. To make the fringed feet, cut a strip of paper the length of your tube and 6cm wide. Fold it half lengthwise. Cut a zigzag pattern along the open edge of the paper through both layers. Glue the central fold along the join of the wrapping paper.

8

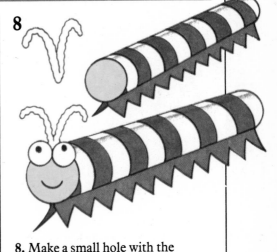

8. Make a small hole with the point of the scissors in the top of the head. Bend the pipe cleaner for the antennae and poke the V-shape into the hole.
For eyes make two paper stones (see page 25). Glue them to the face end and add two dots to the eyes. Draw on the mouth.

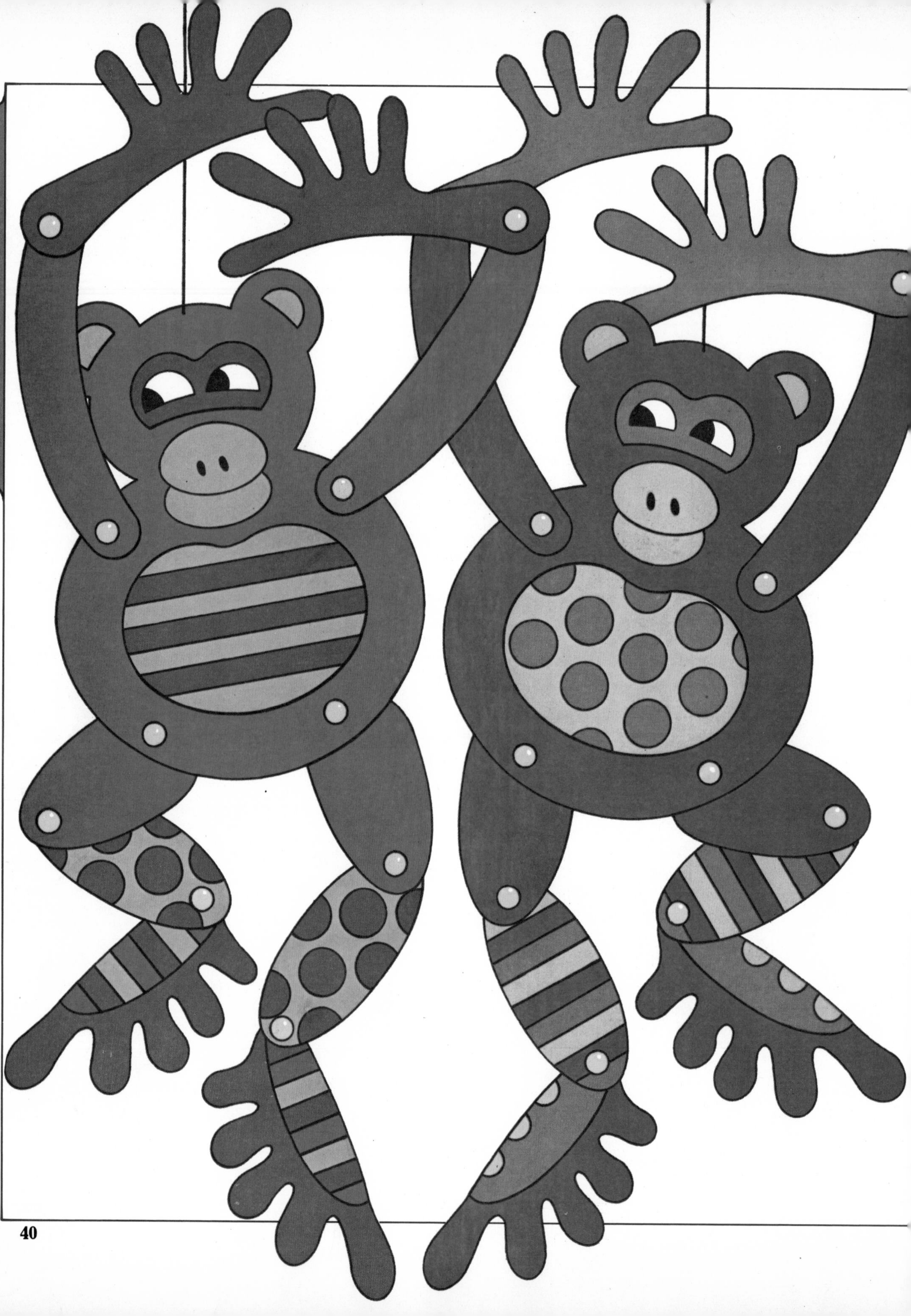

A pair of antic apes

Make this puppet in cardboard and amuse your friends by moving his arms and legs into all sorts of comical positions. Once you have made the monkey you could invent your own animal puppets. Try it first using the pattern below as a trace pattern. This will give you a little puppet about 24cm from finger tips to toes.

▶ You will need:
☐ Sheet of cardboard – a cereal box will do
☐ Tracing paper
☐ Pencil
☐ Paints or felt-tipped pens
☐ Small paper fasteners
☐ Scissors

1. Trace the head and body piece shown below and transfer it onto a sheet of cardboard. Cut it out.
2. Trace the arms and leg pieces shown below and transfer onto cardboard. Follow the diagram on the right. Cut all the pieces out. Letter each piece lightly in pencil on the back.

1
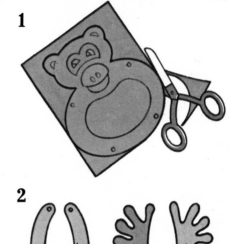

2
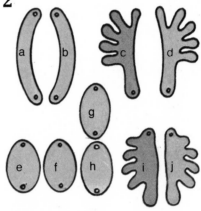

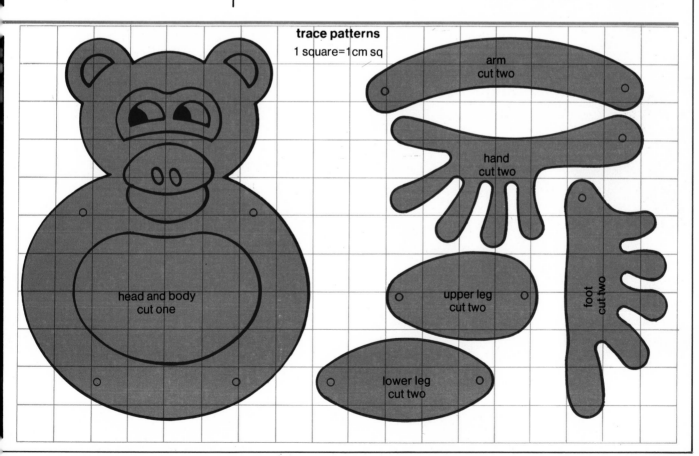

trace patterns
1 square=1cm sq

arm
cut two

hand
cut two

head and body
cut one

foot
cut two

upper leg
cut two

lower leg
cut two

3

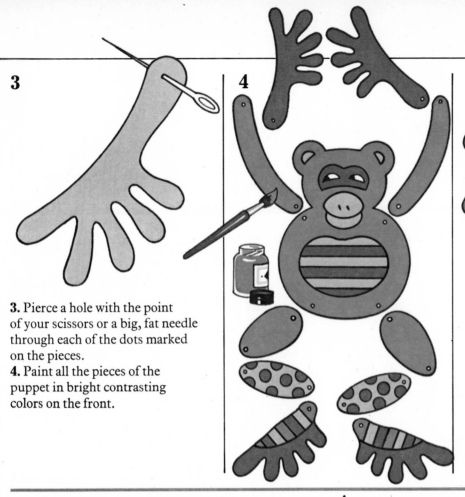

3. Pierce a hole with the point of your scissors or a big, fat needle through each of the dots marked on the pieces.

4. Paint all the pieces of the puppet in bright contrasting colors on the front.

4

5

6

7

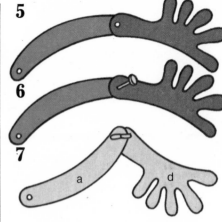

5. Match the hole in one of the arms with the hole in one of the hands.

6. Push a paper fastener through both of the holes.

7. Turn the pieces over and open out the paper fastener.

8

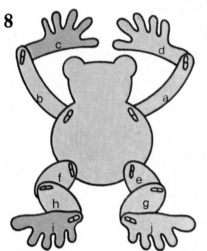

8. Match all the other pieces together and fix them with paper fasteners. The picture above will help you match up the right pieces.

9

9. Pierce a hole in the top of the monkey's head. Put some thread through the hole and tie a knot at the back. Then you can hang your puppet up in different positions.

To make the giant puppet in the photograph, you need to enlarge each of the puppet pieces to scale (see page 4 for instructions on how to enlarge a design). If you enlarge each square on the pattern to 5cm your puppet will be the same size as the one in the photograph on the right. Then follow the 'Try it first' steps 3–8. Make sure you enlarge each piece to the same size. You can make the puppet any size you like.

The finished puppet will look better and last longer if you spray it once or twice with clear varnish or acrylic coating.

Some more trace patterns to fold and cut

These are some more patterns you can trace to make paper cut-outs. See pages 14 and 15 for instructions on how to fold and cut the paper.

All the triangular shapes fit on a piece of paper 18cm x 18cm.